East Germany

At the end of the Second World War, the UK, the USA, France and the USSR divided Germany into zones of occupation. In 1949, the Soviet-occupied eastern zones became the German Democratic Republic (*Deutsche Demokratische Republik*), commonly known as East Germany, and the western zones became the Federal Republic of Germany (*Bundesrepublik Deutschland*), or West Germany.

Since that time, East Germany has developed into an important industrial nation, particularly in the fields of manufacturing and chemicals, and produces a large amount of machinery for export, mainly to the Soviet Union, other east European countries, and West Germany.

There is also an efficient, modern agricultural system.

The country has a socialist constitution, and socialist ideology is the basis of everyday life, at the root of the educational system and the world of work. Industry is almost wholly state owned or run by co-operative enterprise.

In *We live in East Germany*, a cross-section of the East German people, young and old, men and women, tell you what life in their country is like – whether in a town, city, coastal port or country village.

Tim Sharman is a writer and photographer who specializes in recording all aspects of life in East Germany and the other countries of eastern Europe.

BALTIC SEA

Rügen Island

Stralsund • • Göhren

Warnemünde •
Rostock •

Neubrandenburg •

POLAND

Wittenberge •

Gross Ziethen •

River Elbe

Berlin

Potsdam •

River Oder

Magdeburg •

Cottbus •

Halle •

Leuna •   **Leipzig** •

Sömmerda •

Erfurt •   • Krautheim

River Spree

Bautzen •

Meissen •
Dresden •   • Höhnstein

**Karl-Marx
-Stadt** •

Gera •

Seiffen •

Meiningen •

Pöhl •
   • Plauen

Drossdorf •

WEST GERMANY

CZECHOSLOVAKIA

we live in
EAST GERMANY

Tim Sharman

Living Here

We live in Argentina
We live in Australia
We live in Belgium and Luxembourg
We live in Brazil
We live in Britain
We live in Canada
We live in the Caribbean
We live in Chile
We live in China
We live in Denmark
We live in East Germany
We live in France
We live in Greece
We live in Hong Kong
We live in India
We live in Indonesia
We live in Ireland
We live in Israel

We live in Italy
We live in Japan
We live in Kenya
We live in Malaysia and Singapore
We live in Mexico
We live in the Netherlands
We live in New Zealand
We live in Pakistan
We live in the Philippines
We live in Poland
We live in South Africa
We live in Spain
We live in Sweden
We live in the U.S.A.
We live in the Asian U.S.S.R.
We live in the European U.S.S.R.
We live in West Germany

Further titles are in preparation

First published in 1985 by
Wayland (Publishers) Ltd
49 Lansdowne Place, Hove
East Sussex BN3 1HF, England

© Copyright 1985 Wayland (Publishers) Ltd

Phototypeset by
Kalligraphics Ltd, Redhill, Surrey
Printed in Italy by G. Canale & C.S.p.A., Turin
Bound in the U.K. by The Bath Press

British Library Cataloguing in Publication Data
Sharman, Tim
   We live in East Germany. – (Living here)
   1. Germany (East) – Social life and customs
   I. Title   II. Series
   943.1087'8'0922   DD261.2

ISBN 0–85078–551–0

Contents

Birgitt Kissner, *judge*   6

Siggi Treff, *youth hostel warden*   8

Klaus Schröter, *electrician and union official*   10

Johanna Klier, *Olympic athlete and teacher*   12

Wolfgang Nass, *locomotive driver*   14

Eckhard Scharbert, *deep-sea fisherman*   16

Christine Zank, *town councillor*   18

Günter Leichsenring, *toymaker*   20

Iris Grund, *city architect*   22

Kurt Jatzlauk, *bargeman*   24

Ludwig Zepner, *porcelain designer*   26

Dietmar Lippold, *reservoir superintendent*   28

Marion Luttkus, *schoolteacher*   30

Renate Schönfeld, *village pastor*   32

Tomas and Bärbel Porstmann, *medical workers*   34

Uwe Strathmann, *building site director*   36

Lenka Solcina, *Sorb folklorist and performer*   38

Andrea Klepzig, *engineering student*   40

Dieter Martens, *shipyard worker*   42

Cessy Müller, *schoolgirl*   44

Tino Eisbrenner, *rock group vocalist*   46

Prof. Dr Hannes Kästner, *organist*   48

Ria Weimer, *textile worker*   50

Irmgard Peter, *computer assembly worker*   52

Manfred Volkland, *tractor driver*   54

Gerhard Trümper, *building worker*   56

Facts   58

Glossary   59

Index   60

'Crime is not a huge problem'

Birgitt Kissner is 32 and has been a judge for seven years, specializing in family law. Part of her job involves explaining laws and the legal system to the public. She lives in Erfurt with her family.

I sit in a court that specializes in family law, which I like very much. But sometimes it is distressing, particularly with our high divorce rate, and the problems that can create for children. Criminal and labour cases are heard by other judges. Crime, thank goodness, is not a huge problem here. In actual fact it is decreasing, and most of it is just small-scale theft and fraud.

Normally, I am in the court from 7.00 a.m. until midday, hearing cases with two lay judges. They are elected from the local community and have exactly the same rights in court as I do. The rest of my day is spent updating files and making appointments, for even with staff, there is still a lot of administration work that I have to do myself.

I also have to keep up to date with new laws. One important duty of a judge is to go out locally and explain to people how the legal system works, and what the new laws mean. So, often I spend afternoons in schools, or evenings in residential districts, giving lectures and answering questions. This means that I spend less time with my family than I would like.

I have been a judge since 1978, after originally thinking that I would take up teaching. My mother is a teacher and my father a policeman. They both influenced me, but finally law won. I come from a very beautiful little town, Meiningen, south of here in the Thüringian hills. I was very lucky to be accepted for a law course in Berlin, because it is not an easy subject to get into. At university, I was able to express a preference in my studies for the area of law I wanted to specialize in, which was family law. Usually, though, you are directed into the area which most needs people.

Before university, I spent a year working in a solicitor's office, paid for by the state. This was a very useful insight into the workings of the legal system, as well as getting me used to the complex terminology of the profession. Then, after four years at university, I was made an assistant

judge for a year, which is the normal procedure. I had no other duties but to watch, listen and learn. During my studies, I had spent a lot of time in various courts, so the atmosphere was not new to me. What did surprise me, though, was the fixed routine of working life after being a student. Now I am used to this, and run my life accordingly.

I have been married since the first year of my studies. My husband is a teacher here in Erfurt, which is a nice old town, the largest in Thüringia. Fortunately it survived the Second World War without much damage. Because of this, it still has some of the atmosphere of a country town, even though there is quite a lot of industry here now. It is a nice place to live and bring up our two sons, who are now aged 2 and 7.

I am satisfied with my job at present, although how long I do it depends on how well I perform in court, and if I am nominated again by the Minister of Justice, a process that takes place every five years.

The old town of Erfurt suffered very little damage during the Second World War.

Birgitt lives in a flat in this modern block on the outskirts of Erfurt.

'I lost all my hair'

Siggi Treff has been warden at the Höhnstein youth hostel for six years. The hostel is a castle, and very popular. Now 29, Siggi is very happy with the job, enjoying meeting the many visitors.

When I came here to do this job, I was only 23. Many of the staff were older than me, which caused problems for quite a while. In fact, after two years I was ready to run away. That was the period when I lost all my hair! But one group of people here supported me, and so I am still here, enjoying the job enormously. I like contact with young people – so this is the perfect place. We get visitors coming from all over the world, either to stay or just to visit the castle, which has been stuck up here on this rock for 700 years.

Siggi's youth hostel is a 700-year-old castle perched high on the rocks at Höhnstein.

The castle has had a strange history, being used as a prison for centuries and then becoming a youth hostel in 1924. Perhaps its worst period, though, was in the thirties, when it became the first SS concentration camp. There is a small memorial museum here, dedicated to the victims of that time. The first prisoner was the hostel director. Some of the survivors are still around, and they come and talk to the young people here, because I believe that it is important to know what happened in our history.

The hostel is run by the FDJ (Free German Youth) but the area supervisor, my boss, has an office in Dresden and comes down here only a couple of times a year. We are left to make our own decisions and activity programmes, which suits us well. There are thirty-six staff, including builders who are still renovating bits of the castle and converting odd corners to make extra dormitories. All our evening events here, such as concerts, discos and film shows, are open to the local people. We do not isolate ourselves from the village.

It is mostly young teenagers who come here, usually for only three to five days, on what we call activity holidays. They are offered a choice of activities, although we make sure that they are kept busy on all of them. Long walking trips, in the hills and woods around here, are the most popular choice. Our guides are very experienced, and know a lot about the environment in this very beautiful region. It is also particularly suitable for rock climbing, and we run several nature study courses. It is very cheap to come here, costing just a few pfennigs for a bed and five marks for all meals.

A view of the spectacular scenery around the River Elbe, near Höhnstein.

Our reputation for being a relaxed place seems to be spreading. This year we could accept only one in every eighteen kids who wanted to come here, which is why we are adding more bed space. I try to be an approachable warden – it helps that I play guitar and accordion, and can join in the camp fire singsongs, which is how most evenings end.

I always wanted to be a musician, but my father made me learn a trade, so I did an electrician's apprenticeship in Halle, where I was brought up. But that didn't satisfy me, so later on I did manage to go to music school for a year, which is where I met my wife. To work in this business, though, I took a special course, then worked in a Baltic holiday home for a year, before getting the job here. So, here I am, a super job and wife, a nine-year-old son, a nice flat near the village, and a garden plot where I am building a little house for the summer. Life is very good to me.

'New ideas are given high priority'

Klaus Schröter, 60, is a foreman electrician at a chemical plant in Leuna. He is also a union official for the staff of 30,000. Klaus started with the firm as a boy, and will be there until he retires.

This is a huge plant, as big as a town, and it employs 30,000 people. It produces hundreds of basic chemicals and plastics, which are used in many industries and in agriculture. We also export a great deal. The oil feedstock comes from the Soviet Union in a special pipeline.

I come from a farming family, but started an apprenticeship here as a mechanic when I was 15. Now I am a foreman, in charge of the electricity supply to one section of the works. I'm also a shop steward and very involved in the union.

New ideas, to improve production and efficiency, are given a high priority in our industry generally. Since 1977, I have been working on a national committee of the FDGB (Federation of Trades Unions), concerned with innovation. The committee includes people from many industries, as well as scientists. We often visit various plants around the country.

We talk directly to the workers and find that this is where some of the best ideas come from. Useful inventions and changes are rewarded with bonuses, several of which I have had myself over the years. The quality of working life, health and safety has improved greatly since the

Part of the huge chemical plant where Klaus works as an electrician.

Second World War, when most of the plant was destroyed in bombing raids. And, of course, the relationship with the management has changed since it became a state-owned works.

I live near the plant, in a flat belonging to the firm, but most people come by bus from villages and towns up to 50 km (30 miles) away. For this reason, we work four shifts of twelve hours each week, followed by three days off. For most of the workers, it is a job for life, and will be for me, I'm quite sure.

With so many specialist jobs in the place, there are very good facilities for ambitious people who want to retrain or change their job. Many of the top management have worked their way up from apprentices. In the union, we watch out for bright young people. Every year, we sponsor many of them, more than we need ourselves, to go to university. From there, they may go to work in any industry.

At any one time, we have about 2,500

When he is at home, Klaus enjoys playing with his grandchildren.

to 3,000 apprentices learning 36 different crafts, and 200 in a training school preparing for university. We have such a labour shortage in this country that we must do such things. When I became a foreman, I went on a training course thinking that I knew everything, and was shocked to learn of all the problems and responsibilities faced by the management. It was a necessary lesson for me.

Social and sports life in the works is important, and the union is very involved in its organization. We have football teams, bowling leagues, tennis clubs, cycling, shooting, fishing – you name it and we have a club! There is a weekly factory newspaper with a full-time staff. Members of the hobby clubs can get paid leave, if they are very good at their particular hobby, to practise their music, train for sports or whatever. Recently, we sent a young artist to college so that he could study properly. But with my job and union work, I don't have the time for hobbies. When I'm at home, I am just happy to relax or play with my young grandchildren, who live nearby.

'We put great emphasis on sports here'

Johanna Klier, 33, is a former Olympic hurdles champion. She now teaches sport at the teacher training college in Erfurt, and lives with her husband and two daughters.

At the Montreal Olympics in 1976, I won my heats in the 100 metres hurdles. However, I was not the favourite for the final – and I was amazed to find that I won the gold medal. I only believed it after watching the replay. I have a reputation for being cool, but inside I was a bundle of nerves; much more so after the race than before. The result surprised everyone, because I

East Germans are very aware of the value of sport, and many attend exercise classes.

had started concentrating on that event only nine months before the games, after damaging a wrist in one of my other events, shot putting.

You see, contrary to what many people believe, we don't specialize in one event when we are very young. We just train very hard to become generally fit and good at several things, and then see if one begins to dominate the others. I was in the national team, which means in the top five performers, in long jump, high jump and shot, as well as the hurdles.

Coming back to Erfurt from Montreal was also a test of nerves, as there was a big reception for me outside the station. I was presented with flowers, which in itself was funny because in 1968, I had been one of the young girls presenting flowers to other returning athletes. It took a while for my life to settle down after that, but I was married in the same year, and my husband helped me keep my feet on the ground.

Each of the fifteen counties in East Germany has a special sports school for people who show talent. I went to the one here in Erfurt when I was 16. It is very hard work, because you follow the usual syllabus and the sports training is extra, which makes homework a problem. But normal educational standards are not allowed to slip. It was always made clear to me, that a career in sports is very short and therefore you must be able to do something else as well. I chose to study sports science, and that is how I come to be lecturing about sports at the teacher training college. Sport is an important aspect of education here: all teachers must be able to involve themselves in a sport of some

This modern sports centre includes swimming pools, gymnasiums, a roller rink and a solarium.

kind in their school.

Great emphasis is put on sports and general fitness in our country. There are many schools competitions every year – local, county and the national *Spartakiads*, which include all the Olympic events. Generally, facilities are good, but I have seen better in other countries. I am always asked at press conferences what the magic formula is for our international success. All I can say is that an awareness of the value of sport is built into the structure of East German society, and no doubt that combines with our natural sense of discipline, which is necessary for success in anything.

My successes have not brought me any special privileges. My husband and I are living in a nice, but ordinary, flat with our two little daughters who are aged 2 and 5. They are too young yet to know how fast they will be on the track!

'I would love to see the railway restored'

Wolfgang Nass, 31, is a locomotive driver on Rügen Island. The railway is mainly a tourist line, carrying 750,000 people a year. Wolfgang lives in Göhren with his wife.

My father was a fireman on this line, and I was born above the station here at Göhren, right at the eastern tip of the island. When the railway was built, in 1899, the idea was for it to collect agricultural produce and distribute coal. However, it quickly became a tourist attraction, and today, apart from the mail and a few local deliveries, we just carry tourists. The last figures we calculated showed that about 750,000 people ride on the line each year. This is increasing all the time, as more and more holiday homes are built in the area.

The line is 750 mm gauge, and used to run over a dyke to Stralsund on the mainland. Since 1967, it goes only 25 km (15 miles) from here to Putbus, mainly because the rest of the track was in very bad condition and would have cost too much to renew. Locally, the trains are all known as *Dashing Roland*, because their top speed is only 30 km per hour (19 m.p.h.) – and with nine stations and several steep gradients, there are few enough places where we can reach that!

The normal carriages we use are very ordinary and the locos very old. The youngest of our regulars dates from 1925, the oldest from 1913. Recently, we acquired two 1953 machines from a railway near Dresden, and these will be running soon.

We have just rebuilt two carriages in the old style, and are now preparing a loco to match, because this is what the visitors want to see. I have a book on the history of the line, with old maps and pictures, and I would love to see the whole railway restored to its original condition. In those days, the locos were dark green and had names. But although the idea has been discussed, there are no plans to do it yet.

This is a beautiful island and life is very relaxed. But because I was brought up here, I wanted to leave when I finished school, and go somewhere that I thought would be more exciting. So for several years, I worked in Warnemünde as a mechanic. But then I got married. My wife

Wolfgang was born in the station house here at Göhren, on the island of Rügen.

comes from here and didn't want to move, so I came back and worked four years as a fireman, before becoming a driver.

The money is not so good here, but it is cheaper to live and, after all, it is my home and all my family and friends are on the island. There is no doubt that we are different from the mainlanders, and quite proud of it. We always say that a Rügen islander is a rough guy but has a warm heart! And the people are reliable friends, unlike the locomotives, which can be very temperamental. Sometimes, they have to be nursed along as if they were old horses, not machines.

This funfair is on the beach at Göhren, just a short walk from the station.

'I am away for a hundred days at a time'

Eckhard Scharbert has been a deep-sea fisherman all his working life. Recent changes in international law mean that he has to travel further afield before he can fish. He is 44, married and lives in Rostock.

I have no regrets about spending nearly thirty years at sea, but I am not sentimental about it. Maybe, after another few seasons, I will go back to the country and open an inn of some kind. For my wife, that can't happen soon enough! Being married to a seaman is not the best life for a woman, especially when she has young children. The system we work means that I am away for a hundred days at a time, so when I go home to our flat in Berlin, we want to see each other – which means that my wife cannot have a regular job. I earn very good money, though, with all sorts of bonuses and allowances. Recently my son,

Eckhard waits on the quay by his ship, in its home port of Warnemünde, near Rostock.

A view of Rostock and the Warnow estuary looking towards Warnemünde.

who is married with a small baby, has gone to sea after training as a ship's engineer.

When I went to sea in 1956, on smaller boats than there are today, the work was very hard and there were more accidents. There were none of the luxuries that there are now. Sometimes the food was bad, and often we worked for two or three days without sleeping, in cold, rough weather. Over the last twenty years, though, the ships have become bigger and better. Now we work with a large mother ship in every fleet, which means that we get good food and freshly-baked bread.

Of course, it is still not an easy life. We work a twelve-hour shift, but if the weather is really bad and there are problems with winching the nets out of the water, it is literally 'all hands on deck'. I am the first hand, which is like being a foreman, and am responsible for all the winches and cranes. I operate these from the back of the bridge, where there is a good view of the whole deck.

These days, everyone has a proper training, both at a special school and at sea. But there are still some of the old skippers around, who are either sea wolves or philosophers! My skipper is a real old sea wolf, and known in many ports as *Big George*. He worked his way up from the bottom and is rough, but a good skipper.

The biggest change in recent years has been the introduction of an international quota system. This has meant that we must travel further before we can fish. Normally, our first trip each year is to Ullapool, in Scotland, from where we search for mackerel in the North Atlantic. The weather can be terrible up there. Because of the quotas, we often just buy fish from the local fishermen and freeze it on board. At the end of each trip, we take the catch back to Rostock, where there is a large processing plant producing fish cakes and fingers, salted and smoked fillets, rollmops and other specialities.

The trips I like best are to North America, and to West Africa (where the weather is good and it is interesting to go ashore). We have to sell some of the fish we catch locally, because people at home will not eat strange varieties.

'The town council has 220 members'

Christine Zank, 34, is a contact lens maker in Rostock. She is a member of the Liberal Democratic Party, and was recently elected to the town council, where she is involved in looking after public services.

Life has become very busy for me recently. I am the only person in the north of the country making contact lenses. A few months ago, I was elected to Rostock town council, and immediately put on a committee which also involves a lot of work. My father has been an optician here for thirty years. I learned a lot from him when I was young, but was always more interested in becoming a craftworker of some kind. My first choice for a career was decorative ceramics, but I studied to be an optician and then a contact lens maker, and now ceramics is just a very satisfying hobby.

At first, I worked with my father, but four years ago I took over this shop. I had a lot of help from the local branch of the Liberal Democratic Party, who arranged many things with the local council and also helped with the shop conversion. So, when they asked me to join the party, it was difficult to refuse. Then, this year, they nominated me for the town council. The council has 220 members, all local

people from many walks of life.

There are five political parties in the country, the main one, of course, being the Socialist Unity Party (SED), with more than two million members. All the parties, however, have the same major aims.

I was offered a choice of committees to work on, so I selected the one dealing with public services, because these affect everyone. We are responsible for such things as street cleaning, lighting, roads, footpaths and parks. At our last meeting, we discussed ways of motivating people to collect scrap for recycling. It is important to provide different dustbins for each type of waste, and to make sure that people know how to use them. In the new residential districts, we have arranged for one basement room in each block to be kept just for waste paper. To encourage people to save plastic containers, we have put large dump bins outside shops, and now we have huge amounts of material which is sent to factories for reuse.

I am also involved in making sure that

Because of the low birth rate here, a new law was recently introduced, giving privileges to families with three or more children. The privileges include health care, kindergarten, education and holidays. Some councillors visit these families to advise them of their rights, and in a sense, the town becomes a foster parent to them.

Although Rostock is a historic town, it is still thriving, and has many new buildings.

Christine is the only person in the north of the country making contact lenses.

every district has good leisure facilities. Most of the new estates have a sports hall and community leisure centre. Our new tram system, which is still being built, makes it very easy to get into the centre — for specialist shops, cafés and cinemas — or out to one of the swimming pools in the suburbs. As we are near the sea and do not have much heavy industry, Rostock is still a healthy, interesting place to live.

'I am an independent craftsman'

Günter Leichsenring runs the family toymaking business in Seiffen, with his wife and daughter. He is 53 and hopes that his daughter's forthcoming marriage to a toymaker will ensure the business continues.

My great-great-grandfather came to Seiffen as a tin miner in 1834. When the tin was exhausted, he started making toys to sell at the local markets and fairs. Our family has been doing this ever since, becoming, by local standards, quite prosperous.

Normally, toys were made in the winter. The rest of the year was spent working on the land or in the forest. You could say

Günter particularly enjoys making the delicate wooden flowers which are unique to Seiffen.

Large, candle-powered mobiles like this one are a speciality of the Leichsenring family.

special toymakers' school here. In 1945 I went there for three years, before I started working full-time for my family. Soon after 1945, a new law was introduced which helped to encourage the growth of craft businesses with more favourable taxes.

Today, everything we make can be sold quite easily, because of its quality and our reputation; also wooden toys are fashionable in many countries. About 70 per cent are exported, mainly to West Germany, Switzerland and the USA. Although I am an independent craftsman, a co-operative supplies my materials and sells most of my products, but I can also sell from home.

I would really like to make only the things that I like most, such as the delicate wooden flowers that are unique to us. However, large export orders often dictate what is made. We get more realistic prices than in my father's time, so we have been able to accumulate some savings.

As a family, we have our own particular toys for which we are well known. These are all designed and made by myself, my wife, our daughter, and a neighbour who helps out with some of the painting. There are about a hundred registered craftsmen in Seiffen today, but only five who are allowed to call themselves artists. I am proud to be one of them.

There is a very good toy museum in the village, with toys that are over a hundred years old. These still set standards for our work today. I am a member of a village design committee, and we try always to raise the quality of workmanship and ensure that traditional characteristics are not lost. I take great pride in being a Seiffen craftsman, and as my daughter will soon marry a young toymaker, I am hoping that the family business will continue for a few more generations.

that I grew up in the workshop at the back of the house. I can remember, when I was four, operating the lathe with my grandfather guiding my hands.

For a long time now, this valley has been famous for toymaking, and Seiffen is known as 'Toy Village'. There is even a

'My building is called "the finger"'

Iris Grund, 51, has been a city architect in Neubrandenburg since she left university and won a competition to design a new arts centre. Iris feels that the many new buildings in the city make it lack a sense of culture.

When I graduated from university, I was very keen on modern architecture and very much against the old styles. I came to Neubrandenburg because I won a competition to design a new arts centre for the city. This area is fairly flat and there were no high buildings at all; in fact much of the centre had been destroyed in the Second World War. And then along I came and built this tall, thin tower block. There were many protests, and locally it is still

The Stargarder Tor *gate in the old city wall of Neubrandenburg.*

called 'the finger'. It is the only high-rise building in the centre – the rest of the old town has been rebuilt to the same layout and height as before.

I stayed on in the city architect's office after that, working on designs for the new residential suburbs. This was in the sixties, when there was a great increase in the city's population, because new industry was brought to the area as part of the overall plan for the country. Traditionally, the industrial region was in the south, and there were very few jobs up here outside agriculture. Now there are many food processing plants, a tyre plant, and a lot of smaller factories.

The town is not growing so rapidly now, so our building programme is designed to catch up with work that we did not have the time, money or labour to do before, such as building cinemas and cafés.

Although this is an ancient city (the centre still has a wall right around it), what is really missing is a sense of culture because so much is new. Many people have moved here from other districts; they live in suburbs that are almost self-sufficient, so there is hardly any need for them to come into the centre. And a real music lover, like me, must go to Berlin to hear something top class – and that is a long way. However, the big town church, that was to have been kept in a ruined state as a memorial, will soon be rebuilt as a concert hall, which should improve things.

Since 1970, I have been the chief architect here. I work with a team of thirty people, including specialists in urban planning, traffic control, road engineering, restoration and landscaping. So, as well as being an architect, I am a manager.

Iris's tower, known locally as 'the finger', is the only high-rise building in the city centre.

I also deal with committees and even give lectures about our plans, both to local schools and to ordinary citizens.

It is a great responsibility, turning a country town into a modern city, particularly as many people have moved to Neubrandenburg directly from the countryside. But we are not short of land, or water either – we have a very large and beautiful lake nearby. Many families have weekend cottages or summer houses near the lake.

23

'Bargemen can be breathalysed'

Kurt Jatzlauk is 30 and lives in Magdeburg. He is a bargeman, travelling the canals and rivers across East Germany to Czechoslovakia. He is happy in his job, and has no ambition to do anything else.

Sometimes, on a bad day, I think that one day I will meet a girl who will make me settle down; but normally I look forward to becoming an old man in this job. I have worked on barges since I left school in Leipzig, where I was born. I just wanted to travel, so I applied to join the merchant navy. I failed to get in, then soon afterwards I had a letter from the inland waterways people, inviting me to apply to them.

I started my apprenticeship in 1970, spending one year in a training school and one year on a barge. Nowadays they do a sandwich course: three months on the water, three months at school, for two years. It is a very special kind of life, wandering the waterways, and some people don't settle to it – but it suits me, and the money is very good.

To become a skipper, you must spend two years on a barge and then go back to the training school to get a licence for each canal and river, proving that you have been up and down them all at least six times. I got my licence in 1976. It covers me for the River Elbe – from Prague, in Czechoslovakia, to Wittenberge, near the frontier with West Germany – plus all the canals within this country.

My two crewmen and I are based here at the Magdeburg control centre. We normally carry coal from Czechoslovakia down to the gasworks at Potsdam and Magdeburg, and often carry gravel on the return journey. Sometimes, we carry potash to a chemical works – loading that is a very dusty business.

Usually, we travel for fourteen hours a day, which means that when conditions are good, it takes about five days to go upriver to Prague. The only real problem is the changing level of water in the river. Every morning, we get forecasts on the radio. If the level is falling fast, it may be necessary to travel non-stop for twenty-four hours a day, to avoid off-loading somewhere to lighten the barge. The most difficult stretch of the Elbe is between Dresden and Prague, where the river winds through the hills, and there can be

When they are not on duty, Kurt and his engineer enjoy a glass of beer in the barge's cabin.

sandbanks that change position overnight.

Most barges are 80 metres (260 feet) long and can carry 100 tonnes. They are powered by a 420 horsepower diesel engine. New barges are continually being built, and river life today is very busy. I am responsible for the barge and the crew, so I have to be able to do any job on board, including cooking and fixing the engine.

When we are moving, there is no time to relax, as there is a lot of manoeuvring to be done and strict regulations to follow. The river police can stop you for speeding and, because it is forbidden to drink on duty, bargemen can be breathalysed. Some men do travel with their wives and young children, but fewer than in the old days. As for me, I am happy with just my crew-mates and my dog Moppy for company. Moppy has been on the barges with me for eleven years.

This ship-lift raises barges 16 metres (52½ feet) from the River Elbe to the Mittelland Canal.

'A dinner service may take 3 years'

Ludwig Zepner, 53, is design director at Meissen Porcelain in Meissen. He has worked for the firm since he was 15. His job involves travelling, which he finds useful as a source of new decorative ideas.

I came to work here straight from school when I was 15 years old. That was soon after the end of the Second World War – a very interesting time, when the country was experimenting with the new socialist ideas. But although this famous factory is now owned by the state, many of the old Meissen traditions continue.

European porcelain was invented here by Johann Friedrich Böttger. He was actually trying to make gold! With royal approval, he started manufacturing porcelain in the old castle in 1710. Even today, when we know that we can very easily sell any item that we choose to make, there is no question of turning to mass production. It would completely change the image of Meissen, which produces goods for a wide range of tastes, many things being made specially to order.

I started as just an ordinary worker in the moulding department. Then I went for a two-year ceramics course at a technical college, followed by five years' study at art college in Berlin. When I came back here in 1958, I joined a studio developing new designs. However much we depend upon traditional designs, which account for about 85 per cent of our output, I think it is important that every generation should make its own distinctive mark.

Today, there are five people working with me in the studio. We each produce ideas for new items, and also prepare traditional designs for special orders. Something like a huge dinner service, for official functions, may take up to three years to make, depending upon how busy the works is, and how much decoration is involved.

I travel quite a lot, which is valuable as it gives me a chance to see designs in other countries and, just as importantly, new places and landscapes which give me many ideas, especially for decoration. I have recently been to the Far East, and its influences are now finding their way into my work. I have noticed recently that styles in Europe are changing towards more modest classical forms. The period of abstract work, which was rather pretentious, seems to be over.

When I design a tea set, I start by sketching various ideas, then experiment with clay and gypsum models which I make myself. I have to know, of course, all the manufacturing processes, and what it is

Ludwig in his studio at the famous Meissen porcelain factory.

Most Meissen pieces are made to traditional designs, and all are hand painted.

possible or not possible to make. An interesting project that I am working on at the moment is some large, decorative porcelain panels. These will be a feature in the reception area of a new luxury hotel in Dresden. However, such large-scale work does not come along too often.

27

'Water supply is a problem in this country'

Dietmar Lippold, 46, is a reservoir superintendent in Pöhl. His job includes looking after the many visitors to the lake and making sure they do not spoil the area.

We get about 800,000 visitors to the lake each year, including day trippers, campers and holiday-makers. An important part of my job is making sure they respect the lake and its surroundings, because this whole area is a protected nature reserve. There is a large bird sanctuary, and trout breed naturally at the point where a clear mountain stream enters the lake.

Our basic responsibility, though, is to provide water for the towns and industries downstream, from Gera to Leipzig. I am the boss, even though my only qualification for the job is the twenty years I have worked here. I was trained as a mechanic, and worked as a foreman on water supply projects, before coming here when the dam was built.

Building the reservoir was a very expensive project, because apart from the construction work and new roads, compensation was paid to the families who were moved from the little village of Pöhl, which is now under the water. A detailed photographic survey was made of the valley before it was flooded, so that there would be a good historical record of what had been lost.

My duties here are to manage all the

Around the lake are many holiday cabins built by trade unions for use by their members.

personnel and workshops, give technical advice and control the water level by opening and closing sluices. I am also responsible for administration, water quality and the safety of visitors when they are on the water. Water quality is quite good, because there is almost no industry in our catchment area, which might pollute it, and only one small town.

All around the shore are scattered holiday homes and campsites, belonging to unions or factories. In the summer, these are always full, providing me with my biggest headache. The edge of the lake is very easily damaged by visitors, and people on the water often get into trouble, usually due to their own carelessness and inexperience. The lake is 4,000 hectares (10,000 acres) in area and good for watersports, particularly water skiing and windsurfing. Several national championships have been held here.

Water supply is a problem in this country. There is a lot of heavy industry in the cities, needing water, yet rainfall is not very high. In some places, water often has to come from deep boreholes. Pollution laws are very strict. If a factory is shown to be polluting the air or water, the manager can be made to pay a fine from his own pocket, or the whole workforce can lose money from its bonus budget.

Everyone who works here is provided with a house close to the lake, at a very low rent. That suits me because I am a country boy, and I'm used to a home with a garden. My wife is the secretary in a local school. She often complains that if I am not at the lake, I am stuck in my workshop turning wood, which is my hobby. I enjoy it, and it also brings in some pocket money and provides Christmas presents for friends.

The lake covers 4,000 hectares (9,885 acres), and is very popular with windsurfers.

'The school is open from 6.00 a.m. until 5.00 p.m.'

Marion Luttkus is 28 and a science teacher in Neubrandenburg. When lessons are over, many pupils stay on until their parents return from work. Marion runs a microbiology group for them.

I am a teacher in a polytechnic school, where all children go from the age of 6 to 16. My job entails much more than taking a few lessons each day.

I was trained as a chemist and microbiologist. Besides teaching my own subject to the older students, I am responsible for the personal development of my pupils. I am a form teacher – I've had my form for two years now, so we have built up a good relationship and know each other well. And as we all live on the same housing estate, I know their families, and even many of their pets!

Factories and offices start work very early here. It is normal for both parents to work, so the school is open from 6.00 a.m. Some children stay there until 5.00 p.m., when their parents have finished work and, of course, a teacher must be present all the time. The younger children play until 7.30 a.m., then they get a cooked breakfast before lessons start. Lunch is at midday, and school finishes an hour later. But with many pupils staying on, we organize other educational activities. Every afternoon, special groups meet to follow some interest of their own. I run a group studying microbiology – recently they built themselves a very successful piece of apparatus to use for photographing bacteria.

Every month, there is a meeting of the form committee, which consists of the form teacher and about six elected parents. We discuss progress in the class and any problems there may be. Three times a year, there is a meeting for all the parents, when we talk about special plans for such things as excursions and holidays. The pupils have their own meeting with their form teacher twice a month, to discuss social events and to try and solve any problems which have arisen.

All this, of course, keeps me very busy. And I have a husband and two young children at home to look after! But my job does mean that I am very involved with the community – that is what makes the work so satisfying.

Marion lives in a flat here in Oststadt, a modern suburb of Neubrandenburg.

Many of Marion's young pupils go to school at 6.00 a.m. when their parents go to work.

Every year, during the summer holidays, teachers have to go on two-week upgrading courses, to keep in touch with research developments in their field. There is a good genetics centre in Neubrandenburg, so I have specialized in this. I also make sure that I do courses in chemistry because I have to know what is happening in modern research, just in case I ever want to leave teaching and work in industry. Special help with retraining is available for anyone who wants to do this but, at the moment, I do not want to give up teaching. It would be like walking out on my family.

'I am not a pacificist'

Renate Schönfeld, 36, is a pastor in the village of Gross Ziethen. She sees it as part of her job to encourage people to work for peace and justice, and is a member of the peace movement.

I am the eighth generation of Presbyterian pastors in my family. The most important thing about this tradition, to me, is that my two grandfathers were anti-Nazi, and in the thirties my father was in trouble for being a Communist. After the Second World War, in 1945, when we were liberated by the Soviet army, my father embraced the new socialist ideas. I was brought up in an atmosphere that was both religious and socialist, with a belief that

The village shop at Gross Ziethen and, in the background, Renate's church.

society could be both peaceful and just.

I studied theology for five years, joining the FDJ (Free German Youth) and becoming quite active in the organization. It was unusual then for theology students to have such a positive attitude towards our society, as the Church is conservative on so many matters. But if I understand the Bible correctly, the idea is for a better life here and now, not somewhere else in the hereafter. This is the theme of my work in this village as a pastor: not just putting souls to rest, but motivating people to work for peace and justice, both here and in society generally. Groups often come to my house and we sit for hours, discussing world problems, and how Christians should try to live in our society.

I have been here for ten years and seen many changes in village life, particularly houses being modernized. I honestly think that people here are better off, in many ways, than those in towns. What they produce on their private plots of land, for example, is worth a great deal of money to them, and most now have cars.

There is a population of only 350 here now, 30 per cent of them pensioners, whereas there were 800 at the end of the Second World War. The only work available is on the state farm or in a local quarry: there is almost no light work or office jobs. This is why so many have left for the towns, but there is now a trend for young people to stay at home, and it is important that we find good work for them to do.

A very important part of my life is my work in the East German peace movement. I even discuss the subject in church. Recently, our women's group sent a letter

Renate visits the birthday party of one of her parishioners.

to the central peace council in Berlin, expressing our views on world peace. We think it is important that our government knows how we feel about this issue. We regularly collect money in the village, to be sent as aid to poor countries.

Personally though, I am not a pacifist and believe that peace has been maintained in Europe only because the socialist countries have been ready to defend themselves. I also believe, though, that socialist and capitalist countries are both essentially peaceful by nature.

I have been to western Europe on a mission with the peace council, but found it a very greedy and vulgar society. When I was in Paris, I saw hundreds of homeless people living in the Metro. That shocked me; it could never happen in our society.

'Bärbel makes more money'

Tomas and Bärbel Porstmann, 36, are medical workers at a hospital in Berlin. Tomas specializes in transplant rejection, and Bärbel is head of a laboratory analysing patients' samples.

We were in the same year at the Humboldt university, here in Berlin. We met in the FDJ (Free German Youth), and got married in 1971, in our final year. Bärbel comes from Thüringia in the south, where her father was a joiner. My father was a scientist, and he influenced me greatly when it came to choosing what to study.

We both started work here in La Charité hospital directly after university, although in different departments. I did two years as a pathologist, then when I was 26, I served my compulsory two years in the

Tomas at work in his lab at La Charité hospital in Berlin.

army. Fortunately, I was able to work in the military hospital. Bärbel was pregnant while I was in the army, and obviously not very happy about being on her own a lot of the time, and also far away from her family.

Now I am working in the immunology department here in the hospital, looking into the problems of rejection that occur in transplant surgery. I work very closely with the surgeons. This is a field where we do a lot of very good, advanced work here in Berlin. My wife, although working just along the corridor from me, is employed by a different department. It is concerned with the daily care of patients in the hospital, doing routine analysis of samples, using very specialized modern equipment.

Bärbel is head of her laboratory and therefore on a higher grade than me. As she also has the opportunity to work over-time, she makes more money, which she likes to think makes her more important in the family! But we have a good relation-ship and, almost as a hobby, do research together and publish the results in medi-cal journals. It is very important for a scientist to have research papers pub-lished, and it can help your career. But we find the research itself very interesting and satisfying anyway, and there is never a shortage of problems to be solved in medicine.

We live now in a small three-roomed flat with a balcony, in a good area quite close to the centre of Berlin. We had to do a lot of work on the flat to get it the way we like it. Housing can still be a problem here, which is not helped by a high divorce rate. The situation varies from one

city borough to another. Many people, though, do have weekend cottages out in the countryside.

We were lucky in this respect, as my parents had a house in the forest and in 1974, we started building our own cottage in their very large garden. Now we spend most of our weekends there with Romy, our nine-year-old daughter. The basic building was pre-fabricated and rather ugly, so we built a brick shell around it to improve the appearance. As another hobby of mine is working in wood, I have lined the interior with timber, and built everything we needed in the way of furni-ture and storage. Woodwork is good relax-ation after a week's work. But for poor Bärbel, weekends seem to be busier than her week, with cooking and housework — while I enjoy myself in the workshop.

Tomas and Bärbel spend most weekends at the country cottage which they built themselves.

'We will bring more life to the city centre'

Uwe Strathmann is 41 and works as a building site director in Berlin, East Germany's capital. He is currently involved in a city centre redevelopment project on the banks of the River Spree.

I am in charge of this building project, which is one of the biggest and most important in the city today. It is on the site of the very earliest settlement here. The area was almost completely destroyed in the Second World War, so because we have had to dig foundations for the new buildings, we have uncovered a lot of new evidence about people who lived here thousands of years ago.

There was a competition for the design of the project, but in the end ideas from several plans were used, making the church the focus of the scheme. Until a few years ago, the church was not included in the plan, but as it was the oldest building in Berlin, it was decided to rebuild it from the rubble and use it as a museum.

The most important function of this development is to bring a bit more life to the streets of the city centre. It will be a pedestrian area, with narrow cobbled streets leading to the church and lots of small shops, cafés and restaurants. There

will be the usual local shops, but also specialist shops for traditional craftsmen, souvenir places and shops for fashionable clothes. We are also building a chemist's shop exactly in the style of the last century, just to give some atmosphere. And there will be a small bakery with traditional-style ovens.

It is important that the area stays lively in the evenings. The 800 flats that are to be built will help with that. Although most will be occupied by ordinary people, there will be a section with studios for artists, and some flats especially for guest performers at the opera and theatre. The project also includes the restoration of some old buildings, including a beautiful eighteenth-century mansion that will house a restaurant and museum.

It is a difficult job controlling all the different construction activities. Every day brings new problems, but it is exciting to see such a new environment rising day by day. Everything must be completed by 1987, to mark the 750th anniversary of the

A new Berlin suburb, seen from one of the hills built from the rubble of wartime destruction.

official founding of the city. I am happy to say that we are on schedule – I do not anticipate any setbacks because we have a high priority in the city programme.

Previously, I was in charge of building the big *Palast der Republik* just across the river, but before that I was teaching construction techniques in a college in Leipzig. I just thought it would be good experience for a teacher to manage a big project, and applied for the job. I did start my career, though, with two years on a building site, where I learned bricklaying from a fine old craftsman. I always liked technical things when I was at school, and growing up in a country destroyed by war, it seemed obvious to me that I should work in the construction industry.

Uwe's building site in the centre of Berlin, and the rebuilt cathedral.

'Sorb culture is very much alive'

Lenka Solcina, 55, is a Sorb folklorist and performer. Sorbs are a Slavonic people, living mainly in rural south-east East Germany. She lives in Bautzen, but travels widely with the Sorb performers' group.

Before the Second World War, when I was a schoolgirl, the Sorbs were one of the many ethnic minorities in Germany who were persecuted by the Nazis. We were forbidden to speak our own language, but our family always spoke Sorbish at home. I only learned German by playing in the street with other children. In those days I was embarrassed to be different, but now I am glad that my parents clung to Sorb culture, which is so rich and interesting. The Sorbs are a Slavonic people, originally from the far east of Europe. They were amongst the first to settle in this region, which is traditionally known as Lusatia, or Luzica.

Happily, today there is no discrimination at all in the south-east, where most Sorbs live. We have our own schools and colleges, teaching in Sorbish and German. In Bautzen, which is the centre of our culture today, we have our own national organization, the *Domowina*, which publishes books and magazines in Sorbish. All this dates from the time of liberation at the end of the war in 1945. I can remember vividly the excitement when the first troops to arrive were Russian and Polish – fellow Slavs. Suddenly, everyone

A Sorb folk ensemble performing at a festival in the village of Bautzen.

seemed to have the traditional red, white and blue Sorb flag flying from their houses, as if to proclaim their national identity after years of repression.

Since it was founded in 1952, I have worked for the State Ensemble for Sorb Folkculture, first as a singer and lately as a narrator for the many performances that we do both here and around the world. I had always sung in a choir as a girl, but had no formal musical training before joining the ensemble. We have our base in Bautzen, where we keep our archives and rehearse.

We are a travelling company, always on the move from town to town. In the summer, we play at lots of local festivals. Altogether, we do about 180 performances a year, including visits to other countries. My favourite trip was to Indo-China in 1978. We go to many international folk

Stolpen Castle, near Bautzen – the main town of the Sorb people.

festivals, and have even played at the Welsh National Eisteddfod. I have a daughter, who is married now, but she was practically brought up in the group, travelling around everywhere with us.

When I am not touring, I work on plans and programmes for future seasons. I also help with our smaller groups, who perform in villages all around the region. We are subsidized by the state and receive regular salaries. I don't feel that we are specially 'conserved' as museum pieces, because our culture is very much alive. There are many writers, artists and composers creating new works that are definitely Sorbish in character. We always say that Sorbs are tough, with skulls like granite, so I don't see us fading away yet.

'We have a great shortage of labour'

Andrea Klepzig, 24, is an engineering student in Magdeburg. She is working for her doctorate on a project to automate a steel rolling mill. The industry needs to increase productivity and reduce manpower.

I obtained my degree in 1982. Since then I have been preparing for a doctorate in engineering, which takes three years. I am working on a project to automate a steel-rolling mill, in conjunction with a big firm in Magdeburg. Much of the work I do involves computers. Because the technical college here, where I am based, has a research contract with the factory, I am able to use all the facilities of both places, which helps enormously.

Magdeburg is traditionally an area of heavy engineering. Rolling mill machinery has been made here for many years, but for export nowadays we need to produce fully automatic installations, to increase productivity and reduce manpower. Both of these factors are also very important in our own industry, given that we have a great shortage of labour.

Every six months, I have to give a report to my tutor, and every month we have a meeting in the factory to check progress. At the moment, I feel quite good, as I have just handed in one of my reports. I am not the most diligent person, and it is always a struggle to finish them on time. I have visited other mills in East Germany, and although none are yet fully automatic, many are experimenting with new control

Andrea is working on a project to automate a local steel-rolling mill.

40

After the war, the centre of Magdeburg was rebuilt as a pedestrian area.

systems. They are incredibly noisy places to be in, but if the number of people manning them can be reduced, fewer will have to suffer.

When I first went to university, I was interested in many things. Then when the time came to specialize, people told me that electrical engineering was an industry for the future, and I was persuaded to take it up – although the idea was completely new to me. It is not uncommon, though, for women to work in this field. I could have studied in Dresden or Rostock, but they are too far away from Berlin, where my family is. And as my favourite grandmother lives near Magdeburg, I came here. I thought it was a good idea to have one of the family near, without actually living at home. As it turns out, she has been a great help to me, feeding me quite often, and even lending me some money when I was broke.

I share a room in a students' hostel and get a grant of 500 marks a month, which is about half the national average monthly income. The grant includes a 100-mark bonus for having good exam results. I also get an allowance of 500 marks a year for books, which are very cheap here. I have had to make special arrangements to get some foreign technical magazines which are not normally in the college library.

I have been a member of the FDJ (Free German Youth) for a long time, and still work on one or two committees. My favourite pastime is being in a song group which performs folk songs and modern ballads about life in East Germany. That is great fun. When I finish my doctorate, I will work in the Berlin branch of the steel mill firm. I already have a flat there, which is about to be restored, and I am planning to go there soon to furnish it.

'This year we will complete 35 ships'

Dieter Martens, 50, is a ship engine installer at a shipyard specializing in fishing vessels. He is the deputy team leader of a group of fifteen men. He lives in Stralsund, a town on the coast.

I was born here in Stralsund, and apart from the Second World War, when we were evacuated to Rügen Island, I have lived here all my life. My father and grandfather were both plumbers, but I always wanted to work with engines. When I finished school, I started an apprenticeship at the shipyard.

Today I am the deputy team leader of a

This Atlantic freezer-trawler was built at the Stralsund shipyard for the Soviet Union.

group of fifteen men, installing big diesel engines into new ships. It is a tough job. I do a lot of precision measuring, and am also responsible for tuning the engines. Another team follows us, and connects the engine to the propeller shaft.

The biggest problem is coping with any shortage of manpower. During holidays, or when someone is sick, we may end up working with just eight or nine men. The engines come already assembled from Magdeburg. Two of them, each weighing 13 tonnes, go into each ship. And there is not much space to work in, so it is important that we work well as a team. But I am not down in the depths of the ship all day, as I have reports to write and other things to check in the office.

This yard has always specialized in fishing vessels. This year we will complete 33 ships, building the hulls in sections under cover, on three parallel production lines. Most are Atlantic supertrawlers for a long-term contract with the Soviet Union that allows us to plan up to ten years ahead. In the next five year plan, though, we shall also be replacing the whole East German fleet, so there is no shortage of work.

There is no shortage of work when I leave the yard, either, because I am a lay judge in the town and also active in the SED (Socialist Unity Party). Not to mention the yachting club, which is very popular up here on the coast. I have been sailing since I was a boy, and invested my very first savings in a little boat. Later I replaced it with the one I have now: a converted lifeboat in which I installed a cabin and an engine. It is really good for travelling around the coastal islands here.

Dieter is a keen sailor and moors his own boat in the marina beside the shipyard.

But my wife prefers motoring holidays, and this has led to arguments, so sometimes I just go off with a friend. This year, though, we did both go to Soviet central Asia. That was a wonderful trip and enabled me to indulge in my latest hobby, 8 mm film-making. I can tell you, I have spent a lot of money on film this year!

Stralsund is a lovely old town and I am very fond of it. If you look at the town from the sea or the Rügen Island bridge in the evening, its silhouette is marvellous. But as this is a holiday region, the place is packed in the summer. Sadly, the Gothic brick town centre has only been patched up since the war, but now that the new housing programme is almost complete, it should be properly restored soon.

'Some girls say I'm bossy'

Cessy Müller, 16, is at school in Neubrandenburg. She is very keen on sport, and has formed a rhythmic gymnastics group at school. She wants to become a primary school teacher, specializing in sport.

My parents moved here from the south in 1966, mainly because my father was mad about water sports, and there are lots of lakes in this area. He is the director of a construction firm, and my mother works in a bank. I have a sister, Nadia, who is 13 years old. We have lived in this flat since the block was built twelve years ago. It is only a few minutes' walk from my school, where I am now working hard to go to teacher training college. I want to teach sport, plus another subject, at a primary school.

To help prepare myself for this, I am an active member of the FDJ (Free German Youth) group in my class. The FDJ is a very important organization in this country, with members in local and national assemblies. You can join it from the age of 14, after passing a written test about the history and goals of the FDJ movement.

I have built up an FDJ sports group at school, which I have been training in rhythmic gymnastics. This is the sport I'm best at, although I am now too old to become a champion. I did, though, perform at a big festival in Leipzig in front of 100,000 people, which was very scary. My real ambition, now, is to get other people interested in sports. At the moment, I am coaching our rhythmic gymnastics team for a big festival in three years' time. It takes that long to get all the routines perfected. Some girls say that I am bossy! I do like to organize things, but this is all good practice for when I'm a teacher.

One of the best things about school is the out-of-school activities. We go on outings and picnics (when we have to take a parent along); we have discos; we go to films and discuss them afterwards. But it is the expeditions into the forest that I like best, especially when they end up with a barbecue beside a lake, often with a singsong. Every two or three years, the lakes freeze over and then we all go skating, which is great fun.

I am a pop fan and like to listen to lots of new music, mainly on the radio, but at

Cessy's school is in the modern suburb of Oststadt, to the east of Neubrandenburg.

the moment I don't get much chance because I am working very hard at school. I have already applied to a teacher training college, so I must make sure that my marks are good for the rest of the year. But soon our class will start ballroom dancing lessons, which are very popular, and I am determined not to miss out on those.

This year, I was one of only four people chosen from our school to go to a huge peace and friendship youth festival in Berlin. It lasted for four days and was a wonderful experience. We met lots of political leaders and it ended with a *Rock for Peace* concert. When I got home, I was exhausted, and I spent the rest of the holidays in our little cottage by the lake, reading lots of books.

Cessy at home with her mother, and 13-year-old sister, Nadia.

'We need a licence to play here'

Tino Eisbrenner, 21, is the vocalist in a rock group based in Berlin. The band recently had a number one hit. Their ambition is to be taken on by the State Committee for Entertainment, which promotes big televised shows and overseas tours.

There are five of us in our band, *Jessica*. We have known each other since we were very young, living in the same area and going to school together. We always used to listen to a lot of rock music on the radio and play around on different instruments, so it seemed quite natural that we should try and put a group together. The people who really inspired us to perform were

For playing live, each member of the band is paid an hourly rate, with extra for the songwriters.

the British group *The Police*. We saw them on West German television, which we can watch here.

Our first problem was that we had to do our army service. When that was over, we started rehearsing seriously. We tried to do our own songs right from the start, but at first we came out sounding like *The Police* and other groups we admired. Slowly, our own style has developed.

Getting to play in public here is a very complicated business. To play for money, even as amateurs at weekends, it is necessary to have a licence. There are five grades of licence, from basic to professional. The way it works is for a city arts committee to organize a concert, which is also an audition. A jury of established musicians and committee members comes to listen, and awards a licence if they think you are good enough.

We were very nervous when we were trying for our first licence, but obviously someone liked us, because we soon skipped a couple of levels and now we all have 'premier' licences, which are next to the top. But these licences can always be taken away if you play badly. The money a band earns, which is very low at first, is linked to their grade. For each gig we play, we receive a basic hourly rate, with extra for the songwriters, plus allowances for transport and roadies.

Concerts and club gigs are very popular here, but are all officially organized, usually by a town's arts centre or an FDJ branch, never by a private promoter. We have a manager who arranges all the details and also an adviser. The adviser is normally a person connected with showbiz, who is chosen to help plug the band. Our adviser works in television, and arranged some early appearances for us. It was these, plus regular performances on the radio that, in the past year, have enabled us to make a bit of a name for ourselves. We got to number one in both the radio and TV charts with one song.

One nice thing that happened quite by chance, was that a video demo of ours was somehow seen by the makers of the British TV programme *The Tube*, and they actually showed it on the programme. It would be a dream come true if we could play live over there one day!

So, all in all, we are enjoying ourselves, and working hard to improve our music. But there is still a long way to go before we make money and join the ranks of established top groups. For musicians here, the ambition is to be promoted by the State Committee for Entertainment, who promote overseas tours and big televised *Rock for Peace* concerts. We are hoping to play on one of these next year.

'Leipzig has always specialized in organ music'

Professor Dr Hannes Kästner, 54, is the organist at St. Thomas' Church in Leipzig. He tours the world as an organ soloist, and also teaches at the Leipzig Music Academy.

Without doubt, this church is best known for the fact that Johann Sebastian Bach worked here for so many years. I am proud that we are still an important centre of musical life – the most important in the country I would say, although I am sure that Berlin and especially Dresden would claim the same. Although my basic duty is to play the organ for church services and weddings, I have many other responsibilities. We have a choral school here, with a famous boys' choir. I accompany them on frequent tours abroad as well as touring on my own as an organ soloist. As a soloist, I have been to fifty countries, including seven visits to Japan, where the people have a great enthusiasm for European music.

As well as my duties at the choir school, I am a professor at the Leipzig Music Academy. I generally spend ten to fifteen hours a week teaching, depending upon how many organ students there are. Leipzig has always specialized in organ music studies. But even with the academy here,

the best students, the real vituosi, still come and study at the church, as do musical directors who will work in churches with choirs.

There are several hundred regular churchgoers here to St. Thomas' Church but it is full only for festivals, although every Friday and Saturday the choir gives a free concert, and these are always popular. To play the organ in an old Gothic church like this is a wonderful experience and still thrills me. I have played on many beautiful instruments all over the world, but my two here, the light-sounding modern organ and the heavy romantic nineteenth-century organ, are my favourites because I know them so well.

This church is almost like a home to me. After all, I came as a student when I was 10 years old and was appointed organist when I was only 21, which was very young. So, already I have been here many years longer than Bach, who was organist for twenty-seven years. I come from a village quite near to Leipzig, and learned the piano when I was very small. I remember that when I was about 6 or 7, I was allowed to play in the church by the local organist. It was he who encouraged me to come here, to the church school. I have never once regretted it, and would be quite happy to stay in this position until I retire.

Both my family and I enjoy living in Leipzig. It was not badly damaged in the Second World War, and has some very fine buildings, lots of little coffee shops

Hannes at the console of the modern organ in St. Thomas' Church, in Leipzig.

Johann Sebastian Bach was organist at St. Thomas' Church for 27 years, until 1750.

and beer cellars, which give it a good atmosphere. There are also some very good concerts at the new *Gewandhaus* concert hall. The orchestra there is definitely one of the best there is in Europe.

In 1985 we are celebrating the 300th anniversary of Bach's birth. Many events are planned, which means that there will be more visitors than ever to the church and to the city. I will be playing a lot of his music both here and around the world. So, it will be a good year!

'Taxes are very low'

Ria Weimer is 49, and works as a loom operator in a factory making net curtains. Her husband is a maintenance man at the same factory. They live in Drossdorf.

Although I have lived in this house all my life, and come from a farming family, for years both my husband and I have travelled every day to work in a factory that makes net curtains. There are lots of little textile towns in the hills around here. Plauen is by far the biggest, and is famous for its curtains, which are sold to many countries. We go to a new factory, though, that is only 10 km (6 miles) from here. It was built in the countryside, so that village people would not have to travel as far as Plauen every day.

We always work on the same shift. If we're on a morning shift, we get up at 4.45 a.m., see to the animals in the yard — ducks, pigs, rabbits and chickens. We start work at 6.00 a.m. There is a works bus, but it is slow and so we go by car, leaving home at 5.30 a.m. We have breakfast and a hot lunch in the canteen, which saves cooking in the evening, and come home when the shift finishes at 2.00 p.m.

The animals have to be fed again when we get back. In the summer, I may do some gardening, or just sit in the sun for a while with some knitting or mending. In the evening, we spend a lot of time watching television, which often stays awake longer

An angler collects bait at the village pond close to Ria's house.

than we do! We have a colour set with two systems built into it, which means that we can watch two channels of East German TV and three from West Germany. We are very close to the frontier here, and get a good picture. Anyway, if the programme is entertaining, I don't ask where it comes from!

Weaving is traditionally a low-paid job, but today we get bonuses for quality and quantity. Shift workers get extra allowances, so with both of us working we do quite well, taking home about 1000 marks a month each. Taxes are very low, about 60 marks a month, and for a bit extra we get full pay if we are sick.

Every year, we have twenty-three days' holiday. We often go to the Tatra Mountains in Czechoslovakia, or to a union holiday home on the Baltic coast, although this year we stayed at home and decorated the house.

Life in the village is very different now from when I was a girl. We had only eight years of schooling then, with children of all ages together in one classroom. Even as children, we worked on the family farm. I had to help my mother a lot, as my father did not get back from the Second World War until 1948, because he had been taken prisoner. In 1960, the village joined the co-operative farm. We gave our land to it, and my father worked for them. I had started an apprenticeship as a weaver in Plauen back in 1951, and went on to become a loom supervisor, which is what I do now. My husband was originally a joiner, but the money was not good so he retrained as a maintenance man on the looms. When I was young, many people I knew went to the western zone of Germany, as it then was, but I had a good home and family and just felt that somewhere else would be alien. After all, work is work, wherever you do it.

There are many small textile towns in the Erzgebirge Hills; Plauen is the largest.

'A faulty machine can cost me money'

Irmgard Peter, 39, is a computer assembly worker at a factory in Sömmerda. She is on the top grade in her line of work, responsible for assembling all the units and testing the completed machines.

I started working here when I left school, because there are not many jobs to choose from in a small town like this. When the first computers were introduced in the sixties, we all had to be retrained. I found it very difficult, having never seen anything so complicated in all my life. But there were bonuses offered, for those who could improve their qualifications, and better wage scales. So, as I was newly married and needed the money, I stuck at it and eventually reached the top grade for this kind of work.

My job is to finally assemble the computer from units sent from other parts of the factory. I also check all the circuits, and test each machine before it goes to a final inspection department. My monthly bonus depends upon the quality and the quantity of the work I do, and a faulty machine can cost me money.

We still have a conveyor belt system here, with each person in the group assembling a certain part of the machine. But, more and more, we are changing to what we call 'nest' production, where a small team is responsible for the whole assembly process. This makes the work far more interesting, and a lot less repeti-

Irmgard assembles a computer on the production line at the Robotron factory.

This noticeboard outside the factory displays production figures and the pictures of top workers.

tive. This system was developed after discussion with the union, which is very involved with everything in the factory.

There is no compulsion to join the union, but most people do. There are so many advantages, the main one being very cheap holidays. It also organizes all the sports, hobby and social clubs here, which are paid for by the factory.

This plant is the biggest one operated by our company, Robotron, although they have many others in the country, producing electrical goods such as radios, hi-fis and typewriters. This factory has 13,000 workers, who come from all around the district. It produces computers and printers, calculators and radios.

Our most important product today is the computer printer. Most go for export to the Soviet Union and West Germany, although I have seen consignments marked for the United Kingdom. And now we are making the first East German home computer, especially to celebrate the 35th anniversary of the founding of the state. I think it is going to be very popular.

Our flat in the town was built by a workers' co-operative which is partly financed by the factory. They also make craftsmen available for housing repairs and maintenance, which can be very useful. The power plant in the works also makes steam, which is piped to the blocks of flats for heating. So, you see we cannot forget our dependence on the factory in a small place like Sömmerda.

Some people build their own houses and they get free help with things like foundations, as well as favourable loans, but I am happy in a flat and don't want the extra work of a house. I do love our garden plot though – the standard 500 square metres (600 square yards) – which is just outside the town. We spend a lot of time there in the summer, even sleeping in the little summer house that my husband built.

'We are doing well'

Manfred Volkland, 51, is a tractor driver on a co-operative farm in Krautheim. Manfred's family has farmed in Krautheim since 1724, and his three daughters are continuing the tradition.

When I was a boy and all this land was small family farms, most people worked with horses. When someone had a tractor, it was very exciting, and after school we would go to watch. I decided then that one day I would have a tractor. Our family finally got one in 1955. I even thought it would help me to attract a wife – and I was married soon after!

In 1960, the whole village joined the co-operative farm system. After several changes and experiments, the farm has expanded from its original 275 hectares (680 acres). Today it covers 52,000 hectares (128,500 acres) and includes eleven local villages. These are grouped together to specialize in different types of farming.

Here we are arable, growing wheat, barley and oats, which are sold to the state. We also produce vegetable seeds for agricultural use, and for sale to the public. Nearby is a livestock unit with 5,000 milking cows, and in another village just down the road, there is a pig farm with 36,000 animals and a battery house with 340,000 hens. It is all large-scale farming today, with a lot of modern equipment.

Every family still has its own private plot for growing vegetables, and perhaps

Manfred and his wife, daughters and two sons-in-law in their private plot of land.

maize to feed pigs. People keep pigs to eat, or sell them to the abattoir in Weimar. All farm members get some free grain for animals, also turnips and potatoes for themselves.

For many years, I was the deputy and then the chairman of the co-operative, so I was involved in all the changes that have taken place. Frankly, it has been a revolution for us here, and despite a recent wage-freeze, due to problems in the world market, we are doing well. We say now that we don't talk about money, we just have it! I have three daughters and have recently paid all the expenses for two weddings; and last year I bought a new Skoda car. Every year, we go on holiday to a little island in the Baltic. We have done this since 1970, which was the very first holiday my wife and I ever had. It was very strange at first, but we quickly got to like it! I will never forget the first time I saw the sea. I just sat all evening staring at it.

Part of the small village of Krautheim, and, beyond the garden, a small plot of maize.

We could never have gone away if we had not joined the co-operative.

The job of chairman kept me very busy, and in 1968 the doctor warned me that if I continued at that pace, he didn't give much for my chances. So, reluctantly at first, I went back to tractor driving. It wasn't long, though, before I was approached to be chairman of the local branch of the National Front, which is an alliance of our five political parties. This pleased me, because my pride had been hurt a bit, and I like to be involved in village affairs. After all, if you look in the church records, you will find that my family have farmed here since 1724.

Krautheim is only a small place, with just 400 people, but we have several sports teams and a good social life. There is even a modern bowling alley in the new community centre. Although I have three daughters, all working in farming, the Volkland name will continue here, because one of my sons-in-law has adopted the name and, I confess, that pleases me a great deal.

'Our team is like a big happy family'

Gerhard Trümper is the leader of a team of building workers, restoring flats in the Lichtenburg district of Berlin. He is 29 and lives with his girlfriend and her daughter.

A few years ago, it was decided to stop pulling down older districts of Berlin to make room for new apartment blocks, and instead to restore them. Many people preferred the larger rooms of the old buildings and the atmosphere of those streets. Some areas of Berlin still look a bit rough, but now there are teams like ours all over the city, working hard to meet the construction targets set by the politburo. One of these is to fix or replace every old roof by 1988.

I was recruited for this roofing programme when I came back from the Soviet Union, where I had been working on the international 'Friendship' oil pipeline. The first thing I did was to get four colleagues who were with me there, and form a roofing team. We were always looking for ways of doing the job better and more quickly, so we added other tradesmen to the team, who could work alongside us and speed up the whole process. Eventually, this system was adopted generally and is now used in many places.

There are usually about fifteen in our team, including carpenters, plumbers,

Gerhard and his team restore apartments in the old district of Lichtenberg, in Berlin.

scaffolders and bricklayers, as well as roofers. We work only in the Berlin district of Lichtenberg. The way we restore apartments is popular, because we arrange the work in such a way that people don't have to move out. Although we each have our own trade, it is important that if the need arises, any one of us must be willing and able to do another job, rather than wait around doing nothing. This speeds things up tremendously.

I am responsible for everything the team does, including fixing the bonuses and overtime. If someone is hurt, due to safety regulations being broken, I can be punished by the court. I could take a training course to become an area supervisor, but we have such a good spirit in this team, like a big happy family, that I would rather stay with them. And I would get less money if I changed. We do a lot of things together after work, including several nights a week at a sports centre to keep fit. There are a few in the group who I am

teaching to box, in the hope of forming a team for competitions. Boxing is one of my old loves, as I was a national champion when I was younger.

My new love is Renate, and we have been living together for a while now. We have both been married and Renate has a lovely little daughter, Melanie, who is great fun. We were able to do a good exchange with the two flats we had before we were together, and move into one of the restored buildings in our district. The rent, as always in this country, is very cheap and everything was fitted when we moved in – kitchen, carpets, furniture and heating, as well as decoration. So, I expect that we shall be here for a while, although I suspect that one day I shall have had enough of city life and want to go back to my village in Thüringia. That's where I fixed my first roof, on the local church.

After a hard day's work, some of the team go to Gerhard's flat for a drink.

Facts

Official name *Deutsche Demokratische Republik* (DDR), translated as German Democratic Republic (GDR).

Capital city Berlin (population 1,170,000 in 1982).

Languages German. A small percentage of the population are ethnic Sorbs, a Slavonic people whose language and culture has experienced a revival since the Second World War.

Currency The unit of currency is the mark, divided into 100 pfennigs.

Religion Freedom of conscience and belief is guaranteed by the constitution. The State and the Church are separate, and religious instruction is not given in schools but by the various churches to those who seek it. The state does recognize the historical role of various religious movements and in 1983 there were extensive ceremonies marking the 500th anniversary of the birth of Martin Luther, who was born and lived in what is now East Germany. The majority of Christians are Protestants and members of independent Evangelical churches among which the Lutheran creed is dominant. These provincial churches have a congregation of about 7.7 million served by 4,300 pastors. 1.2 million Catholics live in East Germany, mostly in the counties of Erfurt and Dresden. There are forty Free Churches and other religious communities in the country.

Population In mid-1982 there were 16,697,000 people living in East Germany, approximately (23.5 per cent) in rural communities, the rest in towns and cities. The southern foothills are traditionally the most industrialized region with the highest population density; Karl-Marx-Stadt county has 321 people per square kilometre whereas the northern mainly agricultural county of Neubrandenburg has only 57. In 1982 there were 2.9 million pensioners and 3.1 million people under the age of 15. In recent years the typical trend of movement from countryside to town has slowed.

Climate East Germany is in the intermediate zone between the East European continental climate and the westerly airstream of the Atlantic climate. In Berlin the temperature can vary between 30°C (86°F) in summer and −20°C (−40F) in winter.

The mean annual rainfall is about 600 mm (24 inches).

Government East Germany is a socialist state formed after the Second World War from part of the north-eastern region of the pre-war German Reich. It covers an area of 108,179 square km (41,768 sq miles). The new Republic was founded on 7th October 1949. The People's Chamber is the supreme constitutional authority, with 500 members elected every five years. The Socialist Unity Party (SED) is the leading force in society but co-operates with four other parties. The largest mass organizations are the Confederation of Free German Trade Unions (FDGB) and the Free German Youth (FDJ). The State comprises fifteen counties which are subdivided into twenty-eight urban and 191 rural districts.

Housing Large pre-fabricated apartment blocks dominate the centres of the many towns and cities which were damaged or destroyed in the Second World War, and there are also many new and self-contained suburban residential complexes. A new trend is for older city centre housing to be modernized and restored rather than cleared for new apartments. The increase in rural prosperity has led to much modernization of village housing but there are still many examples of traditional buildings surviving in rural districts and small towns. Most housing in the towns is owned by local government or factories and other workplaces, and rents are low. Much rural housing is privately owned.

Education All education is the responsibility of the State and is compulsory between the ages of 6 and 16. It is free of charge and monthly subsistence grants are available to students in higher education. In 1982 there were 172,058 students at 240 technical schools and 130,442 at universities and colleges. Additionally there were 7,800 foreign students registered in East Germany. 92 per cent of children between the ages of 3 and 6 attend the 12,000 nursery schools and 63 per cent of younger children and babies attend a crèche.

Agriculture Despite extensive areas of poor and often sandy soil, East Germany is self-sufficient in basic foodstuffs, having developed an efficient and modern agricultural industry which employs about 10 per cent of the workforce. Since 1945

Glossary

fundamental changes have occurred in the management of agriculture and forestry, commencing with the expropriation of large private estates and the redistribution of land to working farm families. Today all these farms are grouped into co-operatives, there being 1,101 of between 3,000 and 6,000 hectares (7,400–14,800 acres) which specialize in cereals, field crops and fodder production, and another 2,868 concerned with livestock. In addition, there are 479 state-owned farms devoted to research and plant or animal breeding, plus 18 state fisheries.

Industry At the country's foundation, transport systems and raw materials supplies, once a part of a larger state structure, were cut, and major port facilities were lost. Coal and steel traditionally came from Silesia, now in Poland, and the Ruhr, which is now part of West Germany (the Federal Republic of Germany), as is Hamburg, the natural outlet for the main transport river of the region, the Elbe. Also, thousands of factories had been destroyed in the war. From this unpromising beginning East Germany has developed into an efficient industrial society with the highest standard of living of the socialist planned economies of eastern Europe. Manufacturing output is dominated by machine, motor and electrical engineering, and big reserves of potash and mineral salts form the basis of a large-scale chemical industry. Hard coal is virtually exhausted but the country is the world's largest producer of lignite from opencast pits in the south-east, around Cottbus. Finished products are exported worldwide and well-known items include optical equipment from the Zeiss works at Jena, precision machine tools and cameras from Pentacon at Dresden. Much economic activity and scientific research is integrated with the overall policies of the Council for Mutual Economic Assistance (CMEA or Comecon), the socialist equivalent of the Common Market (EEC), of which East Germany is a member. The twice-yearly Leipzig Trade Fair is a well-established and important international event.

Media The political parties, trade unions and youth organizations all publish daily newspapers, the leading daily being *Neues Deutschland*, the official journal of the Socialist Unity Party. There are more than 5,000 specialist and popular periodicals, four national radio programmes and two colour TV channels.

concentration camp A guarded prison camp in which prisoners are held, especially in Nazi Germany during the Second World War.

co-operative An enterprise, such as a farm, which is owned and managed collectively by the employees.

demo Short for demonstration.

genetics The study of the biological ways in which certain characteristics are passed on from parents to their children.

immunology The branch of biological science which studies the ways in which our bodily organisms resist diseases.

porcelain A ceramic material made from kaolin and petuntse (hard paste) or other clays, and other substances such as soapstone and bone ash.

recycle To process something so that it can be used again, waste paper, for example, can be recycled and re-used.

roadies People who are paid to set up a rock group's equipment before a concert and dismantle it after the concert has finished.

socialism An economic system in which the means of production (industries, agriculture, and so on), distribution and exchange (financial institutions) are owned by the community collectively, usually through the state.

Acknowledgement

The author gratefully acknowledges the assistance during his travels of the directorate and staff of Panorama-DDR, Berlin.

Index

agriculture 10, 54
architecture 22, 23
arts 22, 36, 39, 47

Bach, Johann Sebastian 48, 49
Berlin 7, 16, 23, 26, 33, 34, 35,
   36, 37, 41, 45, 48, 56, 57
birth rate 19
boats 17, 24, 25, 43

choirs 39, 48
churches 23, 32, 36, 37, 48, 49,
   57
climate 17, 29
computers 40, 52–3
concentration camp 9
concerts 9, 23, 45, 47, 49
conservation 9, 23, 45, 47, 49
conservation 18
co-operatives 21, 51, 53, 54, 55
crime 6
Czechoslovakia 24, 51

divorce 6, 35
Domowina 38
Dresden 9, 14, 24, 26, 41, 48

education
   colleges 11, 26, 37, 38, 40, 48,
      49
   schools 13, 19, 21, 23, 30–31,
      38, 44, 45, 51
   sports schools 13
   teacher training colleges 12,
      13, 44, 45
   training schools 11, 17, 21, 24
   universities 6, 7, 11, 34, 41
Elbe, River 9, 12, 24
Erfurt 6, 7, 12, 13
exports 10, 21, 40, 53

factories 18, 23, 29, 30, 40, 50,
   52, 53
farms 33, 51, 54, 55
FDJ (Free German Youth) 9, 32,
   34, 41, 44, 47
food 9, 17, 30, 50

gardens 9, 29, 35, 53
grants, student 41

health care 10, 19

holidays 9, 14, 19, 28, 29, 30, 31,
   33, 35, 36, 41, 43, 44, 50, 53,
   56, 57
hospitals 34, 35
hotels 26
housing 9, 11, 13, 14, 16, 18, 22,
   23, 29, 30, 33, 35, 36, 41, 43,
   44, 50, 53, 56, 57

industry
   chemical 10, 11, 24
   computer 52–3
   construction 36–7, 56–7
   electrical engineering 40, 41
   fishing 16, 17, 42, 43
   food 23
   porcelain 26, 27
   shipbuilding 42, 43
   steel 40, 41
   textile 50–51
   toy 20–21

judges 6–7, 43

languages 38
laws 6, 16, 17, 19, 21, 25, 29, 57
legal system 6–7
Leipzig 28, 37, 44, 48, 49
leisure and entertainment 8, 9,
   11, 19, 23, 30, 35, 36, 39, 43,
   44, 46, 47, 51, 53, 55
local government 18, 19
Lusatia 38

Magdeburg 24, 40, 41, 43
markets 20
Meissen 26, 27
military service 34, 37
museums 9, 21, 36
music 9, 11, 23, 39, 41, 44, 46,
   47, 48, 49

Nazis 32, 38
Neubrandenburg 22, 23, 30, 31,
   44, 45

Olympic Games 12, 13
opticians 18, 19

peace movement 33
political parties 18, 43, 45, 55
pollution 29

public services 18
publishing 11, 38, 41

railways 14, 15
religion 32, 33
reservoirs 28, 29
restaurants 36
Rostock 16, 17, 18, 19, 41
Rügen Island 14, 15, 42, 43

salaries 24, 33, 35, 39, 47, 51, 52,
   55, 57
Second World War 7, 11, 22, 26,
   32, 33, 36, 37, 38, 41, 42, 43,
   49, 51
ships 17, 43
shops 18, 19, 36, 49
socialism 32, 33
Sorbs 38, 39
Soviet Union 10, 32, 38, 43, 53,
   56
Spartiakiads 13
sports 9, 11, 12, 13, 19, 29, 43, 44
   45, 53, 55, 57
Spree, River 36
State Committee for
   Entertainment 46, 47
students 6, 7, 40, 41, 48
swimming pools 19

taxes 21, 50
teachers 12, 13, 37, 44, 48
television 47, 50, 51
Thüringia 6, 7, 34, 57
tourism 8, 14, 15, 28, 29
town planning 23
transport 11, 14, 15, 19, 24, 25,
   33, 50

unions 10, 11, 29, 53

water supply 28–9
waterways 24, 25
West Germany 21, 24, 47, 51, 53

youth hostels 8, 9